j796.323 Sil
Silverman, Drew, 1982-
  UCLA Bruins
  30049002794759   DEC   2012

PIQUA PUBLIC LIBRARY
CHILDREN'S DEPT.

DISCARD

UCLA
BRUINS

j796.323 Sil
Silverman, Drew, 1982-
UCLA Bruins
30049002794759

BY DREW SILVERMAN

Published by ABDO Publishing Company, PO Box 398166, Minneapolis, MN 55439. Copyright © 2012 by Abdo Consulting Group, Inc. International copyrights reserved in all countries. No part of this book may be reproduced in any form without written permission from the publisher. SportsZone™ is a trademark and logo of ABDO Publishing Company.

Printed in the United States of America,
North Mankato, Minnesota
102011
012012

 THIS BOOK CONTAINS AT LEAST 10% RECYCLED MATERIALS.

Editor: Chrös McDougall
Copy Editor: Anna Comstock
Series design and cover production: Craig Hinton
Interior production: Kazuko Collins

Photo Credits: AP Images, cover, 1, 12, 17, 18, 21, 23, 27, 28, 42 (top), 42 (bottom right), 43 (top left), 43 (top right); George Long/Sports Illustrated/Getty Images, 4, 7, 9, 42 (bottom left); Rich Clarkson/Sports Illustrated/Getty Images, 11; Ed Widdis/AP Images, 25; Andy Hayt/Sports Illustrated/Getty Images, 31; Eric Draper/AP Images, 33; Mark J. Terrill/AP Images, 34; Victoria Arocho/AP Images, 37; Darron Cummings/AP Images, 39; Brett Wilhelm/NCAA Photos/AP Images, 41, 43 (bottom); Christine Cotter/AP Images, 44

Design elements: Matthew Brown/iStockphoto

Library of Congress Cataloging-in-Publication Data
Silverman, Drew, 1982-
 UCLA Bruins / by Drew Silverman.
     p. cm. -- (Inside college basketball)
 Includes index.
 ISBN 978-1-61783-287-1
 1. University of California, Los Angeles--Basketball--History--Juvenile literature. 2. UCLA Bruins (Basketball team)--History--Juvenile literature. I. Title.
 GV885.43.U423S55 2012
 796.323'630979494--dc23
 [B]
                              2011040003

TABLE OF CONTENTS

DEC 2012

UCLA coach John Wooden, *right*, and center Bill Walton led the Bruins during their glory years in the early 1970s.

PURE DOMINATION

BY JUST ABOUT ANY MEASURE, THE UNIVERSITY OF CALIFORNIA, LOS ANGELES (UCLA) HAS ONE OF THE GREATEST PROGRAMS IN THE HISTORY OF MEN'S COLLEGE BASKETBALL.

Through the 2010–11 season, the Bruins had won 11 National Collegiate Athletic Association (NCAA) Tournament championships. No other school had won more than seven. UCLA had recorded 25 wins in the Final Four. That was eight more than any other program. And since the introduction of the NCAA Tournament in 1939, the Bruins have completed four undefeated seasons. All the other schools in the country have had five undefeated seasons—*combined*.

UCLA has had several periods of success in its history. But no college basketball team has been as successful as UCLA was from 1963–64 to 1974–75. During that period, John Wooden coached the Bruins to 10 championships in

12 seasons. His teams won an NCAA-record seven titles in a row from 1966–67 to 1972–73.

UCLA won 88 straight games under Wooden's guidance between January 1971 and January 1974. That winning streak is the longest in the history of men's college basketball. And many of those wins were achieved in dominant fashion.

The Bruins' best player during much of that streak was 6-foot-11 center Bill Walton. Many consider Walton to be one of the greatest college basketball players of all time. He won 86 games during his UCLA career and lost only four. Walton led UCLA to two championships, in 1972 and 1973. Both came as a part of undefeated seasons.

But Walton was not the only star on his UCLA squads. Henry Bibby was an All-American guard during the 1971–72 season. Keith Wilkes was an All-American forward in the two seasons after that. The biggest star, though, was Walton. He was named an All-American in all three of his varsity seasons. Walton was also honored as the National Player of the Year in all three of those years (1972, 1973, and 1974).

ELITE COMPANY

Through 2011, UCLA has won 11 NCAA Tournament championships. The Kentucky Wildcats are second with seven championships. The Indiana Hoosiers and the North Carolina Tar Heels are third with five, followed by the Duke Blue Devils with four. The Connecticut Huskies and the Kansas Jayhawks have three titles each. And seven schools have won two NCAA championships.

UCLA center Bill Walton pulls down a rebound during a 1972 game against Washington State.

Walton averaged 21.1 points and 15.5 rebounds per game during the 1971–72 season. UCLA went undefeated at 30–0. Walton, who was a sophomore, had 33 points and 21 rebounds during UCLA's 1972 Final Four victory over the Louisville Cardinals. That sent them to the title game. Walton then had 24 points and 20 rebounds in the championship game against the Florida State Seminoles. That 81–76 victory extended UCLA's winning streak to 45. It also marked the sixth straight championship for Wooden and the Bruins. But the five-point win did not satisfy the team's best player.

PURE DOMINATION

BILL WALTON

Bill Walton was known for being somewhat of a rebel in college. As a junior, he was arrested while participating in a rally against the Vietnam War. On several occasions, he publicly criticized US president Richard Nixon and other members of the government. And he spoke regularly about his drug use, as he attempted to seek spiritual enlightenment.

During his 13 NBA seasons, Walton was probably best known for all of his injuries. When he retired in 1987, he held the league record for most games missed in a career. Nevertheless, Walton was productive when he played. In 1977, he led the Portland Trail Blazers to their first NBA title. And he was named the NBA's Most Valuable Player (MVP) the next year. Despite his injury problems, Walton was inducted into the Naismith Memorial Basketball Hall of Fame in 1993.

"We don't like to back into things," Walton said. "We didn't dominate the way I know we can."

The following season, the Bruins went 30–0 for a second straight year. Walton averaged 20.4 points and 16.9 rebounds per game. The junior superstar also saved his best for last.

Walton had one of the greatest games in the history of college basketball in the championship game. He scored 44 points. That set a new record for points scored by a single player in an NCAA Tournament championship game. He made 21 of his 22 shots and added 13 rebounds. UCLA defeated the Memphis State Tigers 87–66. It was UCLA's 75th straight win—and its seventh straight championship.

Some people thought Walton would leave UCLA after that and enter the National Basketball Association (NBA). He was sure to be a top pick in the draft. But Walton declared otherwise on the night of the 1973 NCAA

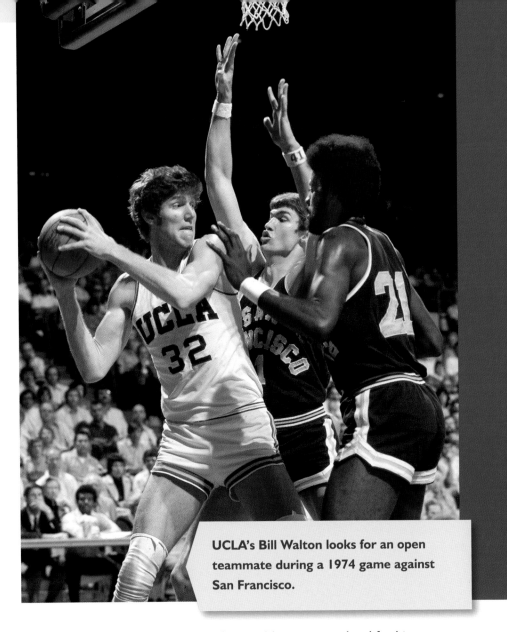

UCLA's Bill Walton looks for an open teammate during a 1974 game against San Francisco.

championship. He announced that he would return to school for his senior season.

"I am not playing pro basketball next year," Walton said. "I have decided there is plenty of time left to earn a living, but now is my time to be a young man."

With their star center back in the mix, the Bruins won their first 13 games in 1973–74. However, Walton was beginning to suffer from a number of injuries. He missed several games early in the season. Opponents soon realized that Walton and the Bruins were no longer invincible.

UCLA's winning streak finally came to an end on January 19, 1974. That day, UCLA led Notre Dame 70–59 with less than five minutes to play. But star forward Adrian Dantley led the Fighting Irish on a run. They scored the final 12 points to stun UCLA, 71–70. Just like that, the streak was over. And for the most part, the Bruins' dominance was too.

"This was great for college basketball," beamed Notre Dame coach Digger Phelps.

The win was one of the biggest in the history of Notre Dame basketball. For UCLA, though, it was just another game—another day in the life of the best basketball program in the country.

NO LONGER INVINCIBLE

The loss to Notre Dame was not the only defeat for UCLA during the 1973–74 season. The Bruins also lost back-to-back games to Oregon State and Oregon in February 1974. And then North Carolina State beat the Bruins in double overtime in the Final Four. In all, UCLA lost four games during the 1973–74 season. That was one fewer loss than the team had suffered in the previous seven seasons combined.

UCLA's Bill Walton posts up against a Notre Dame defender during the Bruins' streak-ending 1974 loss.

"There's no rah-rah stuff about the game," said Bruins guard Andre McCarter. "We look at it like a business, like a job. That's how it is at UCLA."

Before he broke the color barrier in Major League Baseball, Jackie Robinson played basketball at UCLA.

THE EARLY YEARS

UCLA'S BASKETBALL PROGRAM WAS FOUNDED IN 1919. THAT WAS THE SAME YEAR THAT THE UNIVERSITY WAS ESTABLISHED. THE COACH WAS FRED W. COZENS. HE ALSO SERVED AS UCLA'S ATHLETIC DIRECTOR AT THE TIME. THE BRUINS' TEAM CAPTAIN WAS SI GIBBS. IN THEIR FIRST SEASON, 1919–20, THE BRUINS WENT 12–2.

UCLA's first-ever game was a 46–38 win over Manual Arts High School. The Bruins played high schools and various other teams during that first season. That was because they had not officially joined a college conference yet.

That changed the following season, in 1920–21. The Bruins joined the Southern California Intercollegiate Athletic Conference (SCIAC). Led by captain Raymond McBurney, UCLA posted an 8–2 record that season. The mark was good enough to give the Bruins their first conference championship. And the Bruins were just getting started.

YOUNG WOODEN

While Caddy Works was guiding UCLA in the early 1930s, a skinny All-American at Purdue was making a name for himself. The Boilermakers' 5-foot-10, 183-pound point guard was named an All-American each season between 1929–30 and 1931–32. The Helms Athletic Foundation honored him as the 1932 Player of the Year. That same season, he led Purdue to the national championship. The Helms Foundation retroactively named the national champion at the time.

That player was none other than John Wooden. He would later go on to become a college basketball coaching legend at UCLA after leading the Bruins to 10 NCAA Tournament titles during a 12-year period.

Wooden went on to become the first person to be inducted to the Basketball Hall of Fame as both a player and a coach.

UCLA won the SCIAC championship six of the seven years that it was a part of that league. The bulk of those titles came under coach Pierce "Caddy" Works. He took over during the team's third season. Works coached the team from 1921–22 until 1938–39, posting a record of 173–159. The Bruins finished with a winning record nine times in his first 10 seasons. But in his final eight seasons, they did not once have a winning record.

During Works's stint as the UCLA coach, the Bruins had a player named to the All-America team for the first time. That was forward Dick Linthicum. He was recognized as one of the premier players in the country in 1930–31, and again in 1931–32.

However, both of Linthicum's All-America seasons were rough ones for the Bruins. The team ended each season with the seventh-best record in the nine-team Pacific Coast Conference. They went 4–5 in the conference in

1930–31. They then went 4–7 in the league the following year. And things only got worse. Over the next 10 years, UCLA averaged less than two conference wins per season. Meanwhile, they averaged just over ten conference losses per year. The best league record the Bruins had between 1932–33 and 1941–42 came when the team went 4–8 in the Pacific Coast Conference in 1934–35. Simply put, it was not a fun time to be a Bruins fan.

Despite the team's disappointments, UCLA did have some quality players during the 1930s. Seven Bruins were honored as all-conference selections during the decade. Linthicum was an all-league player in 1930–31 and 1931–32. Center John Ball was also picked to the Pacific Coast Conference first team twice, in 1935–36 and 1936–37. The other all-conference performers for UCLA during this time period were forward Carl Knowles (1929–30), center Frank Lubin (1930–31), forward Don Piper (1933–34), guard Don Ashen (1934–35), and forward Bob Calkins (1938–39).

Things got a little bit better for UCLA over the first half of the 1940s. The team posted a 14–7 record in 1942–43. It was the Bruins' first winning season since Linthicum led the 1930–31 team to a 9–6

A FIRST

The first UCLA player to be recognized as an all-conference player was Jack Ketchum in 1927–28. Ketchum, a forward, was the captain of that year's Bruins team.

mark. The coach at this time was Wilbur Johns. He had taken over from Works prior to the 1939–40 season. In 1944–45, the Bruins went 12–12, including a 3–1 record in the league. It was the team's first winning record in the conference since 1927–28. The 3–1 record was good enough to make the Bruins champions of the league's South Division for the first time.

UCLA took a step back in 1945–46. The Bruins won just eight of 24 games. But they turned it around the next season with an 18–7 record and another South Division title. It was by far the most wins in school history. Center Don Barksdale led the team with 14.7 points per game. He was named first-team Pacific Coast Conference and first-team All-American. In addition, Barksdale became just the second African-American player to be chosen as a consensus All-American. The only other was George Gregory of Columbia University in 1930–31.

JACKIE ROBINSON

Jackie Robinson is most famous for breaking the Major League Baseball color barrier with the Brooklyn Dodgers in 1947, becoming the first black player in the major leagues. But he was once a four-sport star at UCLA. One of those sports was basketball. Robinson played on the Bruins' basketball team in 1939–40 and 1940–41. While at UCLA, he was named the Most Valuable Player (MVP) of the Pacific Coast Conference. He led the league in scoring in both of his seasons with the Bruins.

UCLA forward Jerry Norman drives to the hoop during a 1949 game against La Salle. UCLA won 62–57.

In 1947–48, guard Dave Minor was honored as an all-conference performer for the second straight season. Fellow guard John Stanich also was named All-Pacific Coast Conference. But as a team, UCLA struggled. The Bruins finished 12–13 with a 3–9 mark in the league. It would be Johns's final season as the Bruins' head coach. He stepped down to become the school's athletic director. The man hired to replace Johns as UCLA's coach proved to be the right man for the job.

PIQUA PUBLIC LIBRARY
CHILDREN'S DEPT.

THE EARLY YEARS

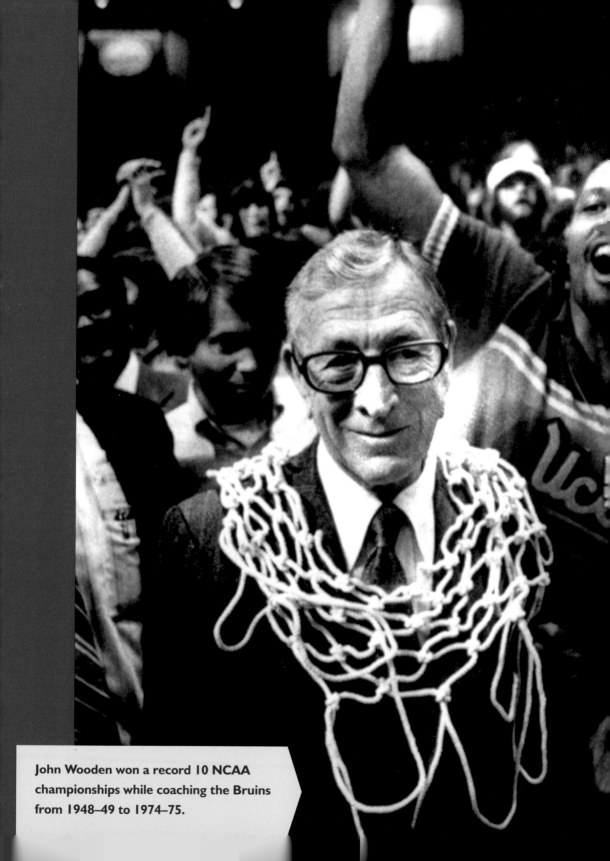

John Wooden won a record 10 NCAA championships while coaching the Bruins from 1948–49 to 1974–75.

THE WOODEN YEARS

THE UCLA BRUINS FINISHED WITH A WINNING RECORD JUST 13 TIMES IN THEIR FIRST 29 SEASONS. NO BRUINS TEAM IN THAT STRETCH WON MORE THAN 18 GAMES. AND ONLY FOUR TIMES IN THOSE 29 YEARS DID UCLA PLACE SOMEONE ON THE ALL-AMERICA TEAM. THEN, WITH ONE HIRE, EVERYTHING CHANGED.

In 1948, UCLA hired Indiana State basketball coach John Wooden. He went on to coach the Bruins for the next 27 seasons. During that time, the team finished with a winning record all 27 times. The fewest wins for any Bruins team in that stretch was 14. And during the Wooden years, the Bruins had 24 All-Americans.

Wooden had unmatched success at UCLA. But the team did not win a national championship during his first 15 seasons with the Bruins. During those first 15 years, UCLA reached the NCAA Tournament only five times. And the team managed a total of just three wins during those five postseasons. Two of those victories came in the 1962 NCAA Tournament. UCLA advanced to the Final Four for the first time in school history that year. It would not be the last.

The Bruins returned to the Final Four two years later. This time, they came away with their first national championship. And they did it in "perfect" fashion. UCLA completed an undefeated 30–0 season with a 98–83 victory over the Duke Blue Devils. Guard Gail Goodrich scored 27 points for UCLA. Meanwhile, guard/forward Kenny Washington had 26 points off the bench. Guard Walt Hazzard added 11 points.

The Bruins did not have a starter taller than 6 feet, 5 inches that season. Instead of height, Wooden took advantage of his team's strengths, such as speed and quickness. The UCLA coach used a full-court press that terrorized the Bruins' opponents. The defense became known as the "Bruin Blitz." It worked very well in the title game. UCLA trailed 30–27 in the first half. But the Bruins used their full-court defense to go on a 16–0 run and take a 43–30 lead. The Bruins never again trailed in the game. And a dynasty was officially underway.

UCLA won its second straight championship in 1965. Goodrich led the way with 24.8 points per game. The senior guard scored a school-record 42 points in the title game against Michigan. UCLA won the game 91–80. That was the final college game for Goodrich. He finished his UCLA career as the school's all-time leading scorer.

UCLA failed to qualify for the NCAA Tournament in 1965–66, even though the Bruins still had an 18–8 record that year. The following

UCLA guard Gail Goodrich dribbles around a Michigan player during the 1965 NCAA championship game.

season featured a major improvement for the Bruins. It began a stretch of excellence that continued for most of the next decade.

Beginning in 1966–67, Wooden guided UCLA to seven straight NCAA Tournament championships. The Bruins lost just five games during those seven seasons. They went undefeated (30–0) three times in that stretch. The first of those undefeated seasons was 1966–67. It was one of the most anticipated seasons in UCLA history. That is because 7-foot-2 center Lew Alcindor was able to play for the Bruins. Alcindor had been one of the greatest high school players of all time. But an NCAA rule at the time barred freshmen from playing on the varsity team. So he had to play on the UCLA freshman team in 1965–66. As a sophomore, Alcindor did not waste time making a major impact.

Alcindor scored 56 points in his very first game. It was a win against one of UCLA's main rivals, the University of Southern California (USC) Trojans. No player in UCLA history had ever scored that many points in a game. And Alcindor did it in his very first game for the Bruins. Later that season, Alcindor broke his own record by scoring 61 points against Washington State.

Teams attempted to stop Alcindor any way they could. They would slow down the game on offense. Then they would double- and triple-team the UCLA big man on defense. But Alcindor always found a way to score. During the 1967 NCAA Tournament, he averaged 29 points per game. And he set an NCAA record by making 66.7 percent of his shots. UCLA won its four NCAA Tournament games by an average of 24 points. That included a 79–64 win over Dayton in the title game.

Alcindor and his teammates had their eyes set on another championship the next season. Senior Mike Warren and junior Lucius Allen both returned as starters in the backcourt. Starting forwards Kenny Heitz and Lynn Shackelford were back as well. With all five starters returning, the Bruins set a school record by averaging 93.4 points per

ALL-AMERICANS

In 1967–68, UCLA had three players selected to the All-America team for the only time in school history. Lew Alcindor, a junior center, was selected to the team for the second of three consecutive seasons. Senior guards Lucius Allen and Mike Warren made the All-America team for the only time in their UCLA careers.

Lew Alcindor scored an NCAA-record 56 points in his first game for the Bruins. It was a 1966 win over USC.

game. Alcindor averaged 26.2 points per game. And he did that even though college basketball players were not allowed to dunk beginning that season.

Alcindor scored 34 points in the 1968 title game as UCLA routed the North Carolina Tar Heels 78–55. Tar Heels coach Dean Smith proclaimed that "Alcindor is the greatest player who ever played the game."

In 1968–69, Alcindor capped his college career by leading the Bruins to a 29–1 record and a third straight championship. He averaged 24 points per game that season. That was down only slightly from his

KAREEM ABDUL-JABBAR

After Kareem Abdul-Jabbar left UCLA, the Milwaukee Bucks selected him with the first pick in the 1969 NBA Draft. He played six seasons for the Bucks and 14 with the Los Angeles Lakers. He won the league's MVP Award six times. And he won six NBA titles—one with Milwaukee and five with Los Angeles.

Abdul-Jabbar retired in 1989 as the NBA's all-time leading scorer with more than 38,000 points. That record still stood in 2011. Abdul-Jabbar's signature shot was the sky hook. It was an impossible shot to guard for most opponents. Abdul-Jabbar was elected to the Naismith Memorial Basketball Hall of Fame in 1995.

26.2 points per game average as a junior. Nevertheless, he poured in 37 points in the national championship game. That helped lift UCLA over the Purdue Boilermakers, 92–72.

Alcindor, who later changed his name to Kareem Abdul-Jabbar for religious reasons, finished his Bruins career as the school's all-time leader in points and rebounds. UCLA won 88 games and lost only twice during his three varsity seasons.

Naturally, there were questions as to who would replace Alcindor once he graduated. Critics wondered if the Bruins could possibly win a fourth straight title. As it turned out, they could.

Junior forward Sidney Wicks stepped up to average 18.6 points and 11.9 rebounds per game in 1969–70. Along with forward Curtis Rowe, center Steve Patterson, and guards John Vallely and Henry Bibby, UCLA went 28–2 in 1969–70. The Bruins topped Jacksonville, 80–69, in the title game. Wicks bottled up Jacksonville's 7-foot-2 center Artis Gilmore that afternoon. The 6-foot-8 Wicks held Gilmore to 9-for-29 shooting and outrebounded him 18–16.

The Bruins won their fifth national championship in a row in 1970–71. Wicks again led the way. He averaged 21.3 points and 12.7 rebounds per game. Rowe also was a major contributor offensively.

The Bruins lost only one game that season. It was an 89–82 loss at Notre Dame on January 23, 1971. But the team would not lose again for more than three years. Wooden and his All-American center, Bill Walton, guided the Bruins to championships in 1971–72 and 1972–73. The Bruins' 88-game winning streak finally ended against Notre Dame on January 19, 1974.

[25]

THE WOODEN YEARS

BRUINS

UCLA lost three more times during the 1973–74 regular season. Then it lost again to North Carolina State in the Final Four. That ended the Bruins' run of seven straight national championships. Said Wooden: "Once we got the game to break the [consecutive wins] record, [the streak] was relatively meaningless. We knew it would end sometime."

UCLA won one more NCAA Tournament championship under Wooden. It came during the 1974–75 season. The legendary coach retired immediately following the 1975 title game at the age of 64. It would be two decades before UCLA basketball won another championship. After defeating the Kentucky Wildcats for the championship in his final game, Wooden said: "I didn't really feel differently about this game. Just very proud."

The old coach had a lot to be proud of. When Wooden stepped down, he left UCLA with a record of 620–147. He won 10

PYRAMID OF SUCCESS

John Wooden's impact on society went way beyond his 10 national championships at UCLA. He developed a Pyramid of Success. It was a layered model for winning at basketball and at life. Wooden became a motivational speaker and a published author. He was a teacher as much as a basketball coach. And Wooden also was known for authoring many famous quotes over the years. Among them were "Be quick, but don't hurry," and "Failing to prepare is preparing to fail." Wooden was known as the "Wizard of Westwood," though he never cared for that nickname. "I'm no wizard, and I don't like being thought of in that light at all," he once said. "'Coach' is fine."

John Wooden stands with Lew Alcindor, *left*, and Sidney Wicks, *right*, after UCLA won the 1969 NCAA title.

championships in his final 12 seasons with the Bruins. That included seven consecutive NCAA Tournament titles from 1967 to 1973. During that stretch, UCLA won 38 consecutive games in the NCAA Tournament. Yet, the record that Wooden was most proud of was the team's 19 conference championships under his watch.

"I thank John Wooden every day for all his selfless gifts, his lessons, his time, his vision, and especially his faith and patience," Walton said. "This is why our eternal love for him will never fade away. This is why we call him 'Coach.'"

Larry Brown won 42 games during his two seasons as the Bruins' head coach. He resigned after the 1980–81 season.

THE POST-WOODEN ERA

IT HAD TO COME SOMETIME. JOHN WOODEN EVENTUALLY HAD TO RETIRE. AND IT WAS NO SECRET THAT THE FORMER UCLA COACH WOULD LEAVE GIANT SHOES TO FILL.

None of the next five coaches to guide the Bruins lasted more than four years. Some of those coaches had success. Two even posted career winning percentages higher than Wooden's. But in the end, it was a long road to get UCLA back to the top of the college basketball world.

Gene Bartow was the first coach to guide UCLA after Wooden. He spent two seasons on the Bruins' sideline. Bartow's first season in charge was 1975–76. He guided UCLA all the way to the Final Four that season. All-American center Richard Washington was the star. Forward Marques Johnson made the All-America team in Bartow's second year. Overall, the Bruins posted a 52–9 record during Bartow's seasons in charge. But as it turned out, the coach and the team were not a good match. "It just wasn't a good job for me at the time," Bartow said years later. "I didn't know that then or I wouldn't have taken it."

Bartow left UCLA after two seasons to take over the program at Alabama-Birmingham. Gary Cunningham replaced him on UCLA's bench. Cunningham also won more than 80 percent of his games with the Bruins. But like Bartow, Cunningham lasted just two seasons at UCLA. Each of those seasons ended with the Bruins ranked number two in the final poll. But this was a school that was used to being number one.

The next coach was Larry Brown. He coached the Bruins for two seasons as well. That included a surprise trip to the national title game in 1980. However, the team lost 17 games combined during those two years. It also failed to win the Pacific-10 Conference either season. The last time the Bruins had gone back-to-back seasons without winning their conference was 1959–60 and 1960–61.

Former UCLA player Larry Farmer took over as coach of the team in 1981. He spent three years on the job. His teams won one conference

ALL-AMERICAN VOID

From 1970 to 1979, UCLA had 13 All-Americans. But between forwards David Greenwood (1979) and Don MacLean (1992), UCLA did not have a single player achieve All-American status. Several Bruins did earn all-conference honors during the 1980s, though. Forward Kenny Fields (1982, 1983, 1984) and guard Pooh Richardson (1987, 1988, 1989) each were All-Pacific-10 Conference selections three times.

Sophomore guard Reggie Miller led UCLA to the 1985 NIT championship over the Indiana Hoosiers.

title (1982–83), but they missed the NCAA Tournament in the other two seasons. Another former Bruins star, Walt Hazzard, was named head coach in 1984. He got off to a rough start. His first team won just three of its first nine games. But the Bruins turned it around. They later earned a berth in the National Invitation Tournament (NIT). That is the second-tier postseason tournament, behind the NCAA Tournament.

UCLA won its first four games in the NIT. That set up a championship game showdown against the Indiana Hoosiers. Bruins guards Reggie Miller and Nigel Miguel scored 18 points apiece in the NIT final. That was enough to give UCLA a 65–62 win. It was the first NIT championship in school history, but the success did not last long.

[31]

UCLA went just 15–14 the following season. The team had not won that few games since going 14–12 in 1959–60. The 1986–87 season was better. The Bruins won 25 games and lost just seven. Miller averaged 25.9 points per game that year. That ranked fourth in the nation in scoring average. Unfortunately for UCLA, the sharpshooting guard graduated after the season. Without Miller, the team quickly sank back to mediocrity with a 16–14 record in 1987–88.

Jim Harrick took over the team prior to the 1988–89 season. He coached UCLA for eight years, but one season stood out above the rest. That season was 1994–95.

The 1994–95 UCLA team featured star forward Ed O'Bannon. He was an All-American and the winner of the Wooden Award, which is given to the best player in the country. The southpaw forward propelled the Bruins to a school-record 32 wins. O'Bannon also led the Bruins with averages of 20.4 points and 8.3 rebounds per game. But it was not O'Bannon who made the shot of the year for UCLA.

The Bruins were playing the Missouri Tigers in the second round of the 1995 NCAA Tournament. UCLA trailed Missouri by one point with 4.8 seconds left. That was when point guard Tyus Edney rescued UCLA. He made an end-to-end dash with the ball, capped by a layup at the buzzer, to give the Bruins the 75–74 victory.

"All I could think about was getting the ball up the court as fast as possible," Edney said. "It was just a great feeling to know that the shot went through and we were still in the tournament."

UCLA senior forward Ed O'Bannon celebrates winning the 1995 NCAA Tournament over Arkansas.

As it turned out, UCLA was just getting started. Edney, O'Bannon, and the rest of the Bruins went on to win their next three games. That set up a showdown with the defending champion Arkansas Razorbacks for the national title.

UCLA suffered a big blow early in the title game when Edney injured his wrist. He was forced out of the game after only three minutes. But O'Bannon and freshman guard Toby Bailey stepped up in his absence. With an 89–78 victory, the Bruins were national champions. It might have taken two decades, but UCLA was back on top.

[33]

THE POST-WOODEN ERA

Steve Lavin coached **UCLA** for seven seasons, but none of his teams made it past the Elite Eight.

MODERN-DAY BRUINS

COACH JIM HARRICK WAS FIRED LESS THAN ONE MONTH BEFORE THE 1996–97 SEASON BEGAN. HE HAD LIED ABOUT A RECRUITING VIOLATION AND WAS DISMISSED FROM HIS JOB. IT WAS JUST 19 MONTHS AFTER HE HAD LED THE BRUINS TO THE NATIONAL CHAMPIONSHIP.

The UCLA basketball community was stunned. Many were just as surprised when Steve Lavin was named as his replacement. Lavin was only 32 years old. That was nearly half the age of the 58-year-old Harrick. Lavin had no head-coaching experience. And he only had two seasons of full-time assistant coaching experience. Yet, Lavin led the Bruins all the way to the Elite Eight in his first season. They had gone that deep in the NCAA Tournament only once in the previous four years. UCLA won 12 straight games heading into the 1997 Elite Eight. However, their Final Four dreams fell short when the Minnesota Golden Gophers upset them 80–72.

The Bruins reached the Sweet 16 four times over the next five seasons. But they were eliminated in that round every time. The Sweet 16 defeats were not pretty, either. In 1998, UCLA lost to the Kentucky Wildcats in the Sweet 16. The final score was 94–68. The Bruins were eliminated in the first round of the 1999 NCAA Tournament. Then Iowa State eliminated them with an 80–56 win in the 2000 Sweet 16. The following year, UCLA lost to the Duke Blue Devils by 13 points in the 2001 Sweet 16. And the Missouri Tigers eliminated UCLA with a nine-point victory in the 2002 Sweet 16.

The pressure was starting to build on Lavin. The 2002–03 season proved to be the breaking point. That year, the Bruins went just 10–19. That included a 6–12 record in the Pacific-10 Conference. It was the most losses for a UCLA team since 1940–41. And it was the team's most conference defeats since 1938–39.

Lavin was fired after that season. His supporters pointed out that Lavin had recruited NBA players to play for the Bruins. But his critics noted that he was unable to lead them deep in the NCAA Tournament.

THE O'BANNON BROTHERS

UCLA forward Charles O'Bannon was named an All-American in 1996–97. Two years earlier, his older brother, Ed O'Bannon, had been named to the All-America team. The O'Bannons are the only brothers in UCLA history to both be named All-Americans. They also were the only All-Americans at UCLA between 1992 (Don MacLean) and 2007 (Arron Afflalo).

Former UCLA coach John Wooden talks to point guard Earl Watson after a 1999 game in the John R. Wooden Classic.

Among the talented Bruins during Lavin's time at UCLA was point guard Baron Davis, a future NBA All-Star. Several other Bruins coached by Lavin went on to have long NBA careers, as well. Among them were point guard Earl Watson and forwards Matt Barnes, Jason Kapono, and Trevor Ariza.

The next coach at UCLA was Ben Howland. He had guided the Pittsburgh Panthers for the previous four seasons. Howland was a native of Southern California. Many considered him to be a good fit for the Bruins. But success did not come immediately for him.

MODERN-DAY BRUINS

UCLA managed only 11 victories during Howland's first season, in 2003–04. That marked the first time the Bruins had posted back-to-back losing seasons since the early 1940s. The Bruins lost a combined 36 games during the 2002–03 and 2003–04 seasons. By comparison, they lost a total of 22 games between 1963–64 and 1974–75.

The Bruins went 18–11 in Howland's second season. They also returned to the NCAA Tournament after two years of not making any postseason tournament. Senior forward Dijon Thompson led the team. But Arron Afflalo, Jordan Farmar, and Josh Shipp provided the big boost. The three freshman guards combined to average 33.3 points, 12 rebounds, and 9.3 assists per game.

The trio of guards returned in 2005–06. They led the Bruins back to the Final Four for the first time since 1995. The Bruins won 32 games in 2005–06, including their first five games in the NCAA Tournament. The sixth game, however, did not go UCLA's way. Afflalo and Farmar combined to make just 11-of-31 shots as the Bruins lost the national championship to the Florida Gators 73–57.

EARLY EXITS

From 2006 to 2011, eight UCLA players entered the NBA Draft before their college eligibility had expired. Jordan Farmar (2006), Arron Afflalo (2007), Russell Westbrook (2008), Kevin Love (2008), and Jrue Holiday (2009) were all first-round picks in the NBA Draft. Three players were second-round picks. Among every NCAA team, only two schools had more players leave early for the NBA Draft during that time.

UCLA guard Jordan Farmar led the Bruins to the NCAA Tournament championship game in 2006.

Shipp did not play in that game. He was limited to just four games that season due to a right hip injury. But he returned in 2006–07 and led UCLA back into the Final Four. That marked the school's first back-to-back trips to the Final Four since 1975 and 1976.

The 2006–07 season ended in familiar fashion for UCLA. The Bruins again ran into Florida in the Final Four. This time, the matchup was in the NCAA Tournament semifinals. But once again, the Gators came out on top. Shipp led UCLA with 18 points. But UCLA's starting guards, Afflalo and Darren Collison, combined to make just 8-of-28 shots in the 76–66 loss.

A STEADY SHIPP

In 2008–09, Josh Shipp became the 15th player in UCLA history to start for the Bruins all four years of his college career. Before Shipp, the most recent four-year starter was Cedric Bozeman. He started at forward for UCLA from 2001–02 to 2005–06 (he missed the 2004–05 season with an injury).

UCLA was back in 2007–08, though. The Bruins reached the Final Four for the third straight year. No team had done that since Michigan State in 1999, 2000, and 2001. Freshman power forward Kevin Love averaged 17.5 points and 10.6 rebounds per game. The backcourt featured a three-guard rotation of Shipp, Collison, and Russell Westbrook. Luc Richard Mbah a Moute was the power forward. It was his third straight season starting for a Final Four team. But UCLA's third consecutive Final Four team was again unable to bring home the championship trophy. The Bruins lost to Memphis 78–63 in the national semifinals.

"As disappointing as this loss is, it's hard to be here three years in a row and not come away with a championship," Howland said.

UCLA remained a solid team after that. Although Love left for the NBA, the Bruins averaged 21 wins and made the NCAA Tournament twice in the next three years. But the Bruins did not get close to reaching the Final Four. Through 2011, Howland had not led UCLA to a title. Nonetheless, fans remember it took John Wooden 16 seasons with the Bruins to capture his first championship.

UCLA forward Kevin Love dunks the ball against the Memphis Tigers during the 2008 Final Four.

On June 4, 2010, Wooden passed away at the age of 99. Through 2011, UCLA had won just one championship since Wooden retired from coaching in 1975. Most Bruins fans, however, believe that the program remains in good hands.

"Coach Wooden was a wonderful person and great friend who is truly a national treasure," Howland said upon hearing of Wooden's death. "His legacy and legend will continue to live on in each of us striving to be the 'best that we are capable of becoming' as athletes, coaches, teachers, parents, and human beings."

[41]

MODERN–DAY BRUINS

TIMELINE

UCLA begins its basketball program.

UCLA joins the Southern California Intercollegiate Athletic Conference.

Junior forward Dick Linthicum becomes the first All-American in the history of UCLA basketball. He earned that honor again the next year.

Jackie Robinson begins his first of two seasons on the UCLA basketball team.

John Wooden, coach of Indiana State University, is hired to take over the program at UCLA.

1919   1920   1931   1939   1948

Alcindor finishes his collegiate career by leading UCLA to a third straight championship with a 92–72 victory over the Purdue Boilermakers.

Led by star sophomore Bill Walton, UCLA posts a 30–0 record en route to a sixth straight championship. An 81–76 victory over Florida State gives the Bruins their 45th straight win and a national title.

UCLA extends its winning streak to 75 by defeating Memphis State 87–66 in the NCAA Tournament title game. Walton scores 44 points on 21-of-22 shooting to propel the Bruins to their seventh consecutive championship.

UCLA loses to the Notre Dame Fighting Irish on January 19. The 71–70 defeat ends the Bruins' NCAA-record winning streak at 88 consecutive games.

Wooden's coaching career ends with a 92–85 victory over the Kentucky Wildcats in the NCAA Tournament championship game. It is the 10th national title in 12 years for Wooden and UCLA.

1969   1972   1973   1974   1975

UCLA reaches the Final Four for the first time in school history.

UCLA defeats the Duke Blue Devils 98–83 to complete an undefeated season. The win gives the Bruins their first NCAA Tournament championship.

UCLA defeats the Michigan Wolverines 91–80 to win a second straight national championship.

In Lew Alcindor's first season with the UCLA varsity team, the Bruins go 30–0 and defeat the Dayton Flyers 79–64 to win the NCAA Tournament.

UCLA places three players on the All-America team, including Alcindor for the second straight season. Alcindor leads the team to a 78–55 victory over the North Carolina Tar Heels in the national championship game.

1962   1964   1965   1967   1968

Star shooting guard Reggie Miller leads UCLA to the NIT championship with a 65–62 win over the Indiana Hoosiers.

UCLA wins its 11th national championship with an 89–78 victory over the Arkansas Razorbacks. Senior Ed O'Bannon leads the way with 30 points and 17 rebounds.

UCLA reaches the Final Four for the first time since 1995.

For the third straight season, UCLA reaches the Final Four only to come up short.

Legendary UCLA coach Wooden passes away at age 99.

1985   1995   2006   2008   2010

QUICK STATS

PROGRAM INFO
University of California, Los Angeles
Bruins (1919–)

NCAA TOURNAMENT FINALS
(WINS IN BOLD)
1964, 1965, 1967, 1968, 1969, 1970, 1971, 1972, 1973, 1975, 1980, **1995,** 2006

OTHER ACHIEVEMENTS
Final Fours: 18
NCAA Tournaments: 44
Pacific-12 Tournament titles: 3

KEY PLAYERS
(POSITION(S); YEARS WITH TEAM)
Lew Alcindor (Kareem Abdul-Jabbar)
    (C; 1966–69)
Lucius Allen (G; 1966–68)
Henry Bibby (G; 1969–72)
Baron Davis (G; 1997–99)
Gail Goodrich (G; 1962–65)
Walt Hazzard (G; 1961–64)
Marques Johnson (F; 1973–77)
Dick Linthicum (F; 1929–32)
Don MacLean (F; 1988–92)

Reggie Miller (G; 1983–87)
Ed O'Bannon (F; 1991–95)
Bill Walton (C; 1971–74)
Mike Warren (G; 1965–68)
Russell Westbrook (G; 2006–08)
Sidney Wicks (F; 1968–71)
Keith Wilkes (F; 1971–74)

KEY COACHES
Jim Harrick (1988–96):
    192–62; 13–7 (NCAA Tournament)
John Wooden (1948–75):
    620–147;
    47–10 (NCAA Tournament)
Pierce "Caddy" Works (1921–39):
    173–159

HOME ARENA
Pauley Pavilion (1965–)

* All statistics through 2010–11 season

The 1966 NCAA Tournament was known as the "Last Chance Tournament" because it was assumed that once Lew Alcindor became eligible for the varsity team, UCLA was going to win the next three championships. And they did.

Steve Lavin was so serious about his defensive teachings that the voicemail on his answering machine ended with the instruction to "Stay in your stance." Under Lavin, UCLA was consistently one of the best defensive teams in the Pacific-10 Conference. The Bruins won at least 20 games six times during Lavin's seven seasons. They also reached the Sweet 16 five times under Lavin, including a trip to the Elite Eight in 1997.

"The most dominant collegiate player of all time in my opinion. An intelligent, graceful, quick, and maneuverable 7–2, unselfish, and a superstar in every sense of the word." —Legendary UCLA coach John Wooden on Lew Alcindor

John Wooden proved that a team could win by being built around African-American players. "At UCLA, we won not just games and NCAA championships . . . but also the minds of those white fans who were skeptical that blacks belonged on America's college teams. . . . What really pushed African Americans to fully integrate was UCLA. [Most] other teams had one black player, maybe two. Coach Wooden had five or six. And they won." —Lew Alcindor

GLOSSARY

All-American
A group of players chosen as the best amateurs in the country in a particular activity.

athletic director
An administrator who oversees the coaches, players, and teams of an institution.

backcourt
The point guards and shooting guards on a basketball team.

conference
In sports, a group of teams that plays each other each season.

draft
A system used by professional sports leagues to select new players in order to spread incoming talent among all teams. The NBA Draft is held each June.

dynasty
A team that maintains its position of power for a long time.

recruiting
Trying to entice a player to come to a certain school.

retire
To officially end one's career. If a team retires a jersey number, no future player is allowed to wear it for that team.

rivals
Opponents that bring out great emotion in a team, its fans, and its players.

seed
In basketball, a ranking system used for tournaments. The best teams earn a number-one seed.

sky hook
A high-arcing shot in which a player extends his arm to the side and brings it back over his head while releasing the ball.

varsity
The main team that represents a school.

FOR MORE INFORMATION

FURTHER READING

Editors of ESPN. *ESPN College Basketball Encyclopedia: The Complete History of the Men's Game.* New York: Ballantine Books and ESPN Books, 2009.

Howard-Cooper, Scott. *The Bruin 100: The Greatest Games in the History of UCLA Basketball.* Kansas City, MO: Addax Pub. Group, 1999.

Wooden, John. *My Personal Best: Life Lessons from an All-American Journey.* New York: McGraw-Hill, 2004.

WEB LINKS

To learn more about the UCLA Bruins, visit ABDO Publishing Company online at **www.abdopublishing.com**. Websites about the Bruins are featured on our Books Links page. These links are routinely monitored and updated to provide the most current information available.

PLACES TO VISIT

Pauley Pavilion
555 Westwood Plaza
Los Angeles, CA 90095
310-825-2101
www.uclabruins.com/genrel/062200aai.html

This has been the Bruins' arena since 1965. The Bruins once went six years without losing a game at Pauley Pavilion, as they won 98 straight games there between 1970 and 1976. Tours are available when the Bruins are not playing.

UCLA Athletics Hall of Fame
325 Westwood Plaza
Los Angeles, CA 90095
310-206-6662
www.uclabruins.com/ot/hof.html

This Hall of Fame and museum features some of the greatest players, coaches, and moments in the history of UCLA sports. The museum includes an assortment of exhibits on John Wooden and his great Bruins teams of the 1960s and 1970s.

INDEX

ABOUT THE AUTHOR

Drew Silverman is a sportswriter based in Philadelphia, Pennsylvania. He graduated from Syracuse University in 2004. He then worked as a sportswriter and editor at ESPN's headquarters in Bristol, Connecticut, before returning back home to Philadelphia. After several years as the sports editor for *The Bulletin* newspaper, he began working for Comcast SportsNet as an editorial content manager.